819.1254 CHR

This
Cockeyed World

ESSENTIAL POETS SERIES 204

Canada Council for the Arts   **Conseil des Arts du Canada**

ONTARIO ARTS COUNCIL
CONSEIL DES ARTS DE L'ONTARIO
50 YEARS OF ONTARIO GOVERNMENT SUPPORT OF THE ARTS
50 ANS DE SOUTIEN DU GOUVERNEMENT DE L'ONTARIO AUX ARTS

Guernica Editions Inc. acknowledges the support of
the Canada Council for the Arts and the Ontario Arts Council.
The Ontario Arts Council is an agency of the Government of Ontario. We
acknowledge the financial support of the Government of Canada through
the Canada Book Fund (CBF) for our publishing activities.

This Cockeyed World

JIM CHRISTY

GUERNICA
TORONTO – BUFFALO – BERKELEY – LANCASTER (U.K.) 2013

Copyright © 2013 Jim Christy and Guernica Editions Inc.
All rights reserved. The use of any part of this publication,
reproduced, transmitted in any form or by any means, electronic,
mechanical, photocopying, recording or otherwise stored in a
retrieval system, without the prior consent of the publisher is an
infringement of the copyright law.

Michael Mirolla, editor
Guernica Editions Inc.
P.O. Box 117, Station P, Toronto (ON), Canada M5S 2S6
2250 Military Road, Tonawanda, N.Y. 14150-6000 U.S.A.

Book design by Jamie Kerry of Belle Étoile Studios
www.belleetoilestudios.com

Distributors:
University of Toronto Press Distribution,
5201 Dufferin Street, Toronto (ON), Canada M3H 5T8
Gazelle Book Services, White Cross Mills, High
Town, Lancaster LA1 4XS U.K.
Small Press Distribution, 1341 Seventh St.,
Berkeley, CA 94710-1409 U.S.A.

First edition.
Printed in Canada.

Legal Deposit – Third Quarter
Library of Congress Catalog Card Number: 2013931301

Library and Archives Canada Cataloguing in Publication

Christy, Jim, 1945-
This cockeyed world / Jim Christy.
(Essential poets series ; 204)
Poems.
Issued also in electronic formats.
ISBN 978-1-55071-717-4
I. Title. II. Series: Essential poets series ; 204
PS8555.H74T49 2013   C811'.54   C2013-900642-7

CONTENTS

End of the World Airfield	7
Heading North	8
'Couver Blues	11
I Had Ears	14
Girl on the Seashore	16
The Heart of the World	17
Head From Mata Hari	18
The Viking's Mother	20
Tomorrow Is Forever	22
Ready or Not	24
This Cockeyed World	25
Lost Channel Road	26
Strong Arm	27
Young at Heart	29
Mute and Staring	30
You and Your Stuff	31
Jim the Drifter	33
Crypto-zoology	35
The Writerly Life	36
Crossroads	38
Freemantle	39
The Juras	41

Knife Fighter	43
Archie Marries Veronica	45
Tucumcari Roadhouse	48
List of Contributors	50
The Lady on Radio Road	52
A Hundred Acres and Some Kind of Fool	56
Strip Bar Haiku	58
Funny Old Memory	59
Wooden Indians	61
Camilo's Bitch	63
And Let the Games End	65
Early Music	67
Even-toed Ungulates	68
Bus Ride	70
One Gaunt White Man	74
Where to, Zoe?	76
Our First Night at the Buchan	80
Big Nicky	82
Greenberg's Drugstore	86
Another Round	88
Runagate Again	91
Tiger Man	95
Afternoon of the Blind Man	96
Guardalavaca Night	98
Forests	99
ABOUT JIM CHRISTY'S PREVIOUS COLLECTIONS	101

End of the World Airfield

Seven planes, all sizes, spread
Over the tarmac after
The storm, like birds
On a white cashmere overcoat.
Undercarriages yellow
Or red, like spoonbills, white-
Tailed kites and ivory gulls.
There's a snowy owl and a common
Tern. One woodcock come out
Of a wood of glass trees. The closest,
Like a pelican, must be
A cargo plane. It's so quiet
You could hear a parachute
Open. Pilots all gone.
Mechanics vanished. Attendants
Wheeled away long ago.
There's no one in the tower.
I'm alone between
Arrivals and Departures,
Next to the coffee machine. It might
Be the end of the world. I
Hear it tell me angels
Have made snow angels
On the runway.

Heading North

I'm headed for Northern Ontario. Nobody'll
Think to look for me there. They'll check
The old familiar southern places they think
My heart still embraces but where I usually
Just got run out of town, or dropped
At the outskirts out beyond the empty multi-
Plex and the last nail salon with an:
"And don't come back."
Atta wa pis kat not Sarawak.
No one'll recognize me under all those
Clothes, I'll be just another Yo-ne-gis
With an icicle hanging from his nose.
My lips will look like a frozen river
Reflecting the grey blue sky.
Things have gotten too hot
In Furnace Falls and I just
Get the blues in Mississippi Station.
I remember the time in Ompah,
Outside the general store when the guitar
Fell on my head and woke me up. I'll
Pass through Tichbourne and claim
To be someone else. You're up there
Somewhere, I know.
I'll find you and take you to Maskara,
Buy you a diamond from DeBeers after
You paint your big brown eyes. I want
To see how you look lying
On a Bear Skin Lake. I'm older
Than you but eager and I'll
Prove it in Summer Beaver.
Ours will be a Marathon love, we'll

Write our names on the Chalk River
And wake up Ati ko kan pledging
Our troth with Caribou bone beats
On mastodon tusks.

>   Webequie
>   Mosonee
>   Moose Factory
>   Let's visit the birds
>   On Akimiski

We'll ride sweet coltsfeet
Along the ice roads, be rash,
Make love behind the leather leaf.
You'll whisper:
>   Wuh nummin Wuh nummin

And tenderly I will sigh:
>   Kitchenuh may koosib

How will that sound at Ear Falls?
Nearby's the Long Legged River
They named after you. Yes,
It calls to me north of Kaba baka.
We'll make camp on the shores of
The big water, you'll say you're
Rescuing the name from an old
English captain, call it after me:
Jim Bay. Let's take the dogs
To Fort Albany, get blankets for
Our antlers. We'll grow old in a lodge
Of skins, paint symbols on the hides:
The sun, the moon, the moose and
Wolverine, animal tracks, tract houses
Of the south. The fires
In our hearts will sketch
Cartoon puffs of smoke
In Northern air. Your giggles
Make the weasel nervous. You'll

Cry 'Pluck, cut, gut' at the snow
Goose. All your stories start:
"This was in the days of Bright
Nose." I especially liked the one
About the cannibal rabbit. One
Night we saw Witikos rise up
Out of the waters, only to be
Defeated by our happiness. We
Will stay there content until you put
The Silver Dollars on my eyes
And send me out in the canoe
Alone, drifting toward the Pole.

'Couver Blues

I'm gonna leave this dreary old 'Couv
Go home,
Pack my grip
And get on the move

Take the passenger train
Far away from all this rain
I'm after bright skies
Want to have to shield my eyes

I'll ride that Hound
   Southern bound
Feel the sand in my shoes
Lose these 'Couver blues

Maybe I'll go to Yucatan
Get a sun tan, won't need no Soleil de Bain
Drink Margaritas with the senoritas
But who am I jiving?
You won't find me at some beach bar
My loonies don't stretch that far

I'd go to FLA
But I wouldn't have the money to stay
Guess I best just head east a ways
Cause I got these 'Couver blues

I could jump in my old Cadillac
Cross the country all the way to Shediac
But the weather's even worse there
And I don't need no Brunswick Blues

I suppose I could try Osoyoos
Breathe some of that dry air
But I don't really like
The kind of people they got there

Maybe go to Alberta
Where I hear a man's free
Under those wide blue skies
At least til they figure how to privatize

I had something happening once
In Moose Hat or was it Medicine Jaw
Least I did until she called the law
And I had to scram
Down to the Badlands
Those kind of memories just make me cry
And I want to keep it dry
I already got the 'Couver Blues

Think I'll cross on into Saskatchewan
I could go to Porcupine Plains
But the women are homely
And the men folk kind of prickly

There's always Weyburn
(Like hell there is)
I've been aiming at Success for years
But they always stop me at the outskirts

Down the road a piece is Oxbow
Where the weather's never inclement
But if I went there I'd just have an incident
I see Old Wives up ahead
But I don't want any of that

Maybe Manitoba's the place for me
Far from all these evergreen trees
Got to get away 'cause I got
These rainy, drizzly, dreary 'Couver Blues

Why not go to Tolstoi
Give away all my possessions
But I'd just get rolled
By Anna Karenina
There's Seven Sisters
And I knew them all but
That's another story

Man, I don't know where I'm gonna go
I got these dripping, mouldy, sniffing
Showers-in-the-morning-increasing-to-rain-
In-the-evening-heavy-at-times,-expect-
Thunder-storms-at-night-with-no-let-up-in-sight
'Couver Blues

But, wait!
Look out the window
Is that the sun
Peeking through?
Yes, it is. And here it comes.
Hey, now!
Everything looks fine
Think I better
Stay right here.
Lose these
'Couver Blues

I Had Ears

Awed I was early on hearing
Their voices in the grooves.
Black LPs icons, not just
Representations but holy
Themselves, and they spoke to me:

"One day Charlie Parker or Thelonious
Monk was walking down the street
And heard …" Jack Kerouac tense
And eager as Saturday morning
On the way to the sandlot, sad
As Gone, in October.

Saroyan, Jack Teagarden's brother,
Who'd been spirited out of Armenia
When their droopy-moustached Papa
Remarried. Same oaken timbre,
Like God, maybe.

Henry Miller from Brooklyn, a cab
Driver, 1937, stopping for coffee,
At the diner on the Edward
Hopper corner.

At first they all seemed to sound
As I wished them. Then Hemingway,
The suburban underwriter boasting
At the white-collar watering hole.
If he was a bouncer
At a whore house in Billings, Montana,
I was the Duke of Windsor.

And Buk who sounded not unlike
His Hem, capering behind the wine
Bottle for all the would-be Buks
Who'd paid their twenty dollars.

Later, I was more prepared for their
Voices. Sylvia Plath's like a hypnotic
Faucet, leaking slowly, drop by drop,
Acid on her Daddy.

Ginsberg on Saturday night, bent
Over cabala and Wichita Vortex
Sutras, singing the schwartza's music
At the back of the synagogue.

And Cendrars on the screen, leaning
Against the bar, like the small-time, big-
Shot of the faubourgs, peeling
One-handed notes from a roll,
Squinting against the dangling butt,
Face like a pelican, squawking
Like one, too.

And from 1890 sickbed, the good
Grey poet, ghastly out of the vault
At Harleigh and Smithsonian,
Sounding his Lionel Barrymore yawp,
Over the rooftops of this cosmos.

I rode the magic ocean of their voices,
Rising on waves, falling
In troughs, dancing in
Combers. The sound of them
Carrying me, goading me
To my own, as just now finished
On the Melbourne stage.

Girl on the Seashore

Entire shell beaches of Paihia
And St. Augustine. Crystal
And Cherry. Horse Conch,
Paua, Abalone. You,
Encountered on those mollusk
Reaches in necklace and bikini. My
Beaded Periwinkle with Shark Eyes
And Bleeding Tooth who let me
Nibble Maculated Baby Ears. Shells
The aggregate that cements us one
To the other. Coquinna and mortar,
En Vida y muerta, Immortal.
My enamorata, my Gaudy
Nautica.

The Heart of the World

I'm on my way, happy
To be going again. Coming back
Maybe never. My passport pages
Are filled with all these
Pretty stamps and visas,
I've got no baggage
To check nor am I carrying on
Any preconceptions.
I do have, however, more dreams
Than can be stowed in the overhead
Compartment or under
The seat in front of me. Oh, I
Can go to Tiflis or, maybe,
Toronto; Hudson's Bay
Or Havana will do but what
I really want to find
Is the place that's not
In the seat pocket by my knees
Or on the map at the back
Of the airline magazine.
Maybe the flight attendant
Can be of assistance.
I press the button and the light
Goes on: "Sir/Madame
Help me, please. I am
Looking for the Heart
Of the World."

Head From Mata Hari

Oh, Mata, Mata, Gretha
Gretha, I boast no gold
Braid nor proud epaulets.
No fruit salad spilled
Across my chest. I don
Only the poet's uniform.
So thank you even more
For the afternoon at the Meurice,
For fitting me in between
Generals. But it's me
Who will be there proclaiming,
Before the white wigs, you
Pure, pristine as sands of
Java beaches of young
Womanhood, near the temples
Where you danced. See, I
Even believe the lies you
Believe, which is the secret
Of your profound sincerity. I
Apologize for everything that
Came later, except for loutish
Garbo in that movie. The fine
Officers deserted you, Mata,
And so too your Russian, but
Not me, I who cradled
Your corpse on the killing ground.
Ah, Mata,
Your graying hair tucked
Under the tri-cornered hat
Like dust under a rug. The
Run in the cheap stockings

They allowed. The two nuns
Wept. That night, like the secret
I was, I sneaked into the Institute
Of Anatomy and stole
Your severed head, and have
It still.

The Viking's Mother

He had no memories of Oslo, though when
Drunk, drew ghost pictures and, deep
In his cups, pillaged and worse in
Skin-sided towns along rugged
Coasts. He was steadfast
In the kitchen in a Viking ship
As it coursed through his bloodstream. Then
He'd thrust his chin out like that prow. At such
Times he wielded his stories like Tyr
With a broadsword keeping Celts
Away or any half-Italian intruders who
Might want to make it a conversation. When he
Got like that his wife escaped to the bedroom.

He was a little better when he'd only
Had a few, and recalled his father, the Resistance
Hero that smote Nazis from the saddle
Of a big snorting Norton, and dismounted
In leathers to conquer women of the far fjords.

Worst was when sober and only then
Did he mention the mother who'd lain
Low his hero with whatever it took. It
Wasn't pretty though she
Was, he had to admit. He'd torn
Up all her photos but kept his father's
In his wallet. There he was seated
In an armchair looking to the right
Like Whistler's mother, no rope taut
Muscles but a belly and the tv remote,
And the one of the fabled motorcycle:
A .250, no chopper.

So the mother, a harridan must be
For sure, by now, I figured, with
Perms and pomades to ward off
Cruel time's tricks on one-time
Vamps. But then she arrived
In Toronto and we went to
Meet the train, me standing off
So as not to intrude, and the one
He's hugging must surely be
An older sister, a comely
Surprise to fool his buddy. I looked
Beyond them for some stout party
Harrying the porters. But, no, this
Was indeed the Viking's mother, still
Only mid-forties. And she came
Forward, each stride like tearing
Silk. We got in the back
Of the taxi, she and I,
And her hand was on my leg
With Union Station still in the side
View mirror. We stopped
At the Summerhill Liquor Store
And the Viking went in for whiskey. She
Turned her head and her tongue
Was in my mouth, my hand under
The skirt of the Viking's mother.
"Here he comes," she said, pulling away.
"You can get the rest of it later."

Tomorrow Is Forever

The wind rattled across the plains
Like the devil's own icy breath,
And the demons inside made him turn south.
The Stars and Stripes gave an angry salute
And the border post resembled
A patriotic two-holer. The pair
Inside were too cold to come and look.
Soon there was the town and an hour later,
The woman, neither of whom he'd seen
In thirty years. And it turned out the latter
Owned half the former but you can't play
Sam Spade in a place like that so
He just walked into one of her offices. "I knew
You'd come back some time," she said,
And looked at him the way Claudette Colbert
Looked at Orson Welles in that movie when
The penny dropped. The rest of them pretended
Not to be paying attention when their boss
Told the stranger she didn't have anyone, that
She'd be off in an hour and a half, and he should
Come by the house, a big white affair with green
Roof and shutters, last house before the border.
Then she told him where Ronee worked and
That he should go and take a look at her; tell
Her or not; either way, he had her blessing.

Ronee had eyes like waifs in velvet
Paintings but she was a big girl with a pair
Of studs in each ear and no wedding ring. She
Looked like country music singers ought to look.
Maybe she went out with ranchers

Who wore jeans and boots and listened to
Merle Haggard. Maybe she
Scraped their backs with those
Long nails. He took the form that Ronee
Gave him, saying he'd fill it out and bring
It back later. Maybe he'd leave hints
Between the lines or tell the entire tale
In the space for "Additional Comments".

He walked into that same coffee shop
And it was like June, 1968 all over again,
Them looking at him, and he expected
One to say to another: "That's the fella's
Been keeping company with Millie runs
The Dairy Queen." He remembered
Getting up from his candy apple red
Vinyl counter stool and going to meet Millie,
Driving her car to the borderline where they
Tore at each other's clothes, like kids
At Christmas wrapping. When he took
His foot off the clutch, the old Ford bucked
Like it was coming out of chute number two.

He finished his coffee and got out
Of there and drove north. There was the big
White affair with the green roof and shutters.
Last house before Canada. Lights were
On and Millie was waiting for him behind
Those curtains. Ronee probably there
With her. He slowed the car but
Just couldn't do it so he
Kept on driving.

Ready or Not

No, no! Stop!
Mama, Mama, please don't
Scream. Stop pushing, relax.
Eat ice cream. Nibble a pickle.
Get even fatter. I liked it like
That. Like this. My current
Residence; it's perfect. Couldn't
Be beat. Plenty to eat here. Warm.
No worries. No job. No teachers.
No unemployment lines. No
Rejection letters or fist fights
In alleys at the back of bars.
No angry lovers, no bad music.
I've even gotten used to father's
Weekly thrusts. So, mama, please
Please get up from the Joe Weider
Incline Bench, your birthing chair
Of choice. Birth me not, Mama
Stop that pushing this instant.
No more of that screaming. I wish
To stay right here
In a cozy ball.
Can't you understand that,
Mama?
Shit.
Here we go
And, oh, it's cold.
And our screams are one,
Mama.

This Cockeyed World

Red brick houses burst from the snow
Like boutonnieres from lapels
Of your white, cashmere benny.
You were here once in the same snows
At the house on Gothic Avenue. We
Rode taxis to pharmacies clear
To Parliament for Benze-Dex
Nasal inhalers that you crushed
Into Rye and Sevens. Yesterday, I
Repeated stories you told me:
About the tap-dancing cuckold
And the man who fell in love
With a trolley car. They laughed
At the coffee shop, here on a planet
Still turning. A new kind of scene
Where even an old rounder such
As you has a place in a corner, however
Remote, of the World Wide Web. World
Where jazz is deader than
The Diving Horse, every co-ed
Has a tattoo and dope fiends have
Taken over middle management.
So sleep the long sleep,
Your junkie bones meal
For Jersey rats.

Lost Channel Road

A thick-flake snow, like
Laundry detergent, light,
And just enough to clean
The grey from winter
Fields crowding Lost
Channel Road. A Blue
Jay still hanging about
The farm yard, worrying
Chipmunks, looking with rue
Upon the thorny ash; too poor for
Flying south to join its rough-
Voiced scrub mates in Florida.
Me, too. In car now, crossing
Carrs Road, headed to frozen
Stoco Lake.

Strong Arm

Just around this boutique corner
It's still there, the Strong Arm
Club: windows plywood
Cataracts; weeds and phlox
In the parking lot; original
Sign still flexing its muscle.
The dancing biceps girl
A faded outline in blue. The things
We got up to inside, Indian
And white. Guys skidding
On their rears across linoleum
Like novice ice skaters. And the band
Never missed a beat. The guy
I didn't know, waiting outside
Behind the door. The boot's
Steel toe on my thigh, thick
Fist with death head's ring.
Just because he'd staked a claim
On the Indian woman who
Wanted no part of him. When
It was done, a few minutes later,
I went back in for the sheer or-
Nery-ness of it, found her and we
Danced again, pushing with our
Bellies, and walked out
Together, me ready and waiting,
Flinging open the door because
I was fast and twenty-seven
But he had gone, skulking –
I like to think – down Dovercourt.
And we turned, holding each other

Tight, passing under the brand new
Strong Arm sign, with the bright
Blue dancing biceps girl.

Young at Heart

The big window's a movie
Screen and she just walked
Out of the past, criss-crossing
Into the sunshine.
Started up six steps with legs
Of noirish molls; the Forties' kicks
And thrift store pillbox, half
Her forehead veiled; a woman
Twenty-eight. The guy, not the man
She deserves, and dressed like
A little boy who's stolen a bottle
From the liquor store, twelve pigeons
Roosting in the eaves, and opened
The door. What's she doing with
Him? I feel like calling out, "Hey!
What about me? I should be
Your man." And it might have
Been – was – me, once
Upon a time. But if she passed
Me on the porch and even noticed,
I'd be but the weird, old gold-
Toothed guy lives in the basement.
And now I know longing
Is tactile. And "You're only
As young as you feel"
Just another one
Of Life's big lies.

Mute and Staring

I saw a pangolin today, rocking
Side to side like a sailor
Burdened by his armour.
The thing stopped to sniff
At cracks in the hardpan, and I
Watched it carry on toward
A roebuck deer like a cutout
On a far off ridge. And before
The little monster got there
A black curtain descended
And someone turned on
African stars. All I could do
Was stand there mute
And staring.

I saw a pangolin today, therefore
I won't be in to work tomorrow. In
Fact, you probably won't see
Me for a longtime, if ever. Maybe
Mr. Hawking can tell me what
This burrowing thing has to do
With black holes and big bangs.
But I have a feeling he doesn't
Know, either. It's just another
Thing to try and figure out but
I'm way behind already

You and Your Stuff

Dawn wore a guilty look; coming
In the window, as if ashamed
For being gone so long. You
Followed it through the door
A heartbeat later, chewing gum
Without a care in the world, and
Even more time had passed
Since you'd been around.

Dawn's lips were like
A bruise, yours a lipstick smear.
Bedraggled, the both of you.
I knew where *It* had been but
You I didn't ask. You might
Have told me.

You took the last coffee from
The pot and I went outside
To check the car I bought you,
That little Cruiser Convertible I'd
Thought you'd look so cute in. I
Was worried about the bumpers
And the fenders.
But it wasn't there. And I told myself
I'd had enough,
And went back inside
To throw your stuff in the street,
And you after it.

You were sitting on the edge
Of the bed, skirt up, unrolling
Those old-fashioned stockings.
The way you lifted that leg and
Pointed that foot. Well what's
It all about anyway and what
Matters and what doesn't? I'm
Not getting any younger, after all,
And I can always throw your stuff
And you out some other time.
There will be other times.

Jim the Drifter

Had me a traffic stopper once,
Boys, when I was a Prince
On the Royal Road. She caused
Alarm clocks to do Stromboli
All over town, and forget about
Ingrid Bergman. My door bell
Was a gamelan orchestra
When she hove into view.
Why my horse up and died
At the thought of her
Riding him, and crossing
The Avenue she turned two Toyotas
Into an art installation. The woman
Made Dolores del Rio look like Fatty
Arbuckle. First time we met
I started speaking Latvian.
She was even better looking
Than Hank's last wife.
And ...
        Well, hell, it wasn't that way
At all. She was okay, I suppose, but
Nothing other than many another
Fading moll of the mini malls. Too
Many cigarettes and tortilla chips. Too
Much CC and Seven. At her best, two-
Stepping, she probably resembled
A redneck's notion of Cleopatra,
And mine, too. And that's what
She left me for, some roofer on
Parole or a guy who sold
Tractor parts. But I was never

Any prince of the world on any
Royal Road, just another fool
On the Lost
Highway.

Crypto-zoology

The creature was dead on the beach
In the raw Newfoundland cove, big
And white, and resembling nothing
Else. It looked left over from
A sand castle competition, willy-nilly
Made by nihilists with buckets,
Plastic shovels and no plan
But God's. It had long white
Hair, coarse and tangled. Experts
Flew in and pronounced the thing
A whale, and the coarse, tangled,
Long white hair, cartilage. And
Flew away.
And the young fishermen
With hardly anything to do,
And the old timers with even less, stared
At the thing and knew better because
They had been out in those dark
Grey waters and looked in the face
Of other mysteries.

The Writerly Life

The old ones always resemble
The audience at folk concerts
And the singers look just
Like them but their own
Work has no music. Smug
With tenure, well-known writers
No one else has ever read.

The young ones with hot drinks
More complicated than the hendecas
They might have heard about
In second year, looking up
To see if anyone's watching them
At their laptops. Blank faces over
Blank pages. Writers of the coffee
Shop not the maelstrom.

Who are these people and when
Did everything change? What became
Of the drunks and dreamers, the
Roisterers who fired pistols in the street,
Worked the oyster beds and logging
Camps, drove cab and slung hash
In order to buy a few nights to rip
The hands from the clock,
Open a vein behind a locked door, spin
The carriage and crumble page after page?
Who risked everything and wouldn't
Sip just a single organic, micro-brewery
Brew, and for a piece of ass grant
Letters of recommendation; who conducted

No workshops, chaired no committees
And Tweeted
Not?

Crossroads

Went down to the Delta
Just like Robert Johnson done
But in a rental SUV, facial
Hair as careful as topiary.
Need him that Explorer jussa
Hold his video gear.
Got out at the Crossroads,
Axe like a quiver 'cross
His back, new Robin Hood
Hero of the Blues. Got it
All on tape, sounding like
Howlin' Wolf, at least until
The playback; doing awkward
Little Walter moves; signifying,
Like he thought Son House
Would do. Looked all around
Fo' dat Debil, wanting to make
Any kind of deal. And three
Young men on their field hand
Holiday roared by, rap rumbling
Their convertible, and laughed
At this pale fool, for the devil
He don't make no deals
With no boy down
From Toronto
On no Council Grant.

Freemantle

Too long cosseted
In that cottage of stone
Along the estuary, days
Of Turner-type light,
And nights the mistral cavorted
Like a ghost in the chimney, and
Embers were fireflies.
I was content with my Aramaic
Declensions and old postcard
Collection: tinted views
Of Maracaibo before the wells,
And the slave market of ancient
Saint Augustine.

Too long cosseted,
For one night while the Red
Wolves wailed, I found the ebb
Had lain old Lanky Bob on shore.
His left foot gone and most
Of his nose, and a Spot Viper
Curled inside the familiar Samoan
Shirt, its short teeth gripping
Bob's right nipple as if it had
Held on for the ride.
Yet how artfully the serpent
Fused the inked panoply that
Was Bob's manly chest: the
Russian stories that spoke only
To those in the know; women,
And jokes in Basque; the

Dead Man's Hand; and nine
Years in that joint in Belgium,
Reduced to a few inches
Just below the clavicle.

How he'd found me was both
Mystery and miracle, and I hoped
It would stay that way, though
I figured Albanians were involved;
They usually are. But the appearance
Of Lanky Bob signaled my time
Cosseted was done, just as sure
As those embers were ashes now.
So I left him where I found
Him, his one bloated foot pointed
At Freemantle, and I lit out
For the Territories.

The Juras

Thumbing in the Juras, nearly
Forty years ago. In cluses,
Like valleys between breasts,
Sleek green carpet fields, and towns
Of watchmakers who dreamed still
The dream of anarchism. I
Caught a ride from a guy who
Took me home to meet his folks.
They lived in a blood-red A-frame
And he might have been
My lost milk brother, the one who'd
Gotten the best of it when they
Separated us at the mid-wife's
In Neuchatel. He didn't draw
The grown-ups who scrapped
The live-long day, cursed
Communists and all dusky peoples.
No uncles with size thirty-eight calibre
Waists. His aunts did not
Take numbers.
He got the big-hearted ones, that
Laughed, kept goats and ducks.
Had a Nubian daughter-in-law,
And a sloe-eyed cousin my age.
Grandfather had never been
A party hack but he'd known
Kropotkin personally, had him
Over to the house, "And he'd sit
Right there where you're sitting now,
Taking notes for Daily Bread."
They gave me a room of my own,

Right next to my good milk
Brother and across the hall
From the cousin. "You
Might as well have that old Audi
Out in the barn. Stay as long as
You wish." And I might have,
In that house with the steep-
Pitched roof poking like
A blood red 'A' between
Breasts of the Juras.
But everything, finally, was
Just too easy, so after a week
Of it, I stuck out my thumb
Again, for I was intent
On going down
A harder road.

Knife Fighter

You weren't waiting after
Midnight in a trashcan alley
And I didn't come stumbling
Drunk as Silenius, jangling
Car keys and a pocketful
Of change.

Nor were you lean and steely-
Eyed, like a veteran of these
Encounters and the only visible
Scar was of a different kind,
Like a tire track across
Your lower abdomen that I'd
Come to know so well.

You had on next to nothing, so
Where you hid the shank, I'll
Never know but it might as
Well have been a ground-
Down shard of tin with
A black-taped jailhouse
Handle.

You didn't close in, edge
Up, shifting it from hand
To hand, sliding left
And right. It just went
In between the ribs
On the left side and you
Gave it a twist
For the hell of it.

I never saw it coming, my
Arms being around you at
The time and you were
Laughing like a hyena
In a dirty blond wig.

Now others, truth be
Known, may have tried
Something similar. But
They hesitated or the blade
Was dull or they didn't
Approach the job with
The proper spirit. You
Obviously had experience.

Well I watched as the corpse
Stayed on the ground and
Eventually this other thing
That looked just like it, got
Up and walked away, after
About a dozen years. And now
It goes about its business
Looking for someone to
Whom to show
The scar.

Archie Marries Veronica

He appeared in the late-Depression,
The eternal juvenile lead. And
With that apple pie blonde
And the other one who wasn't
Wholesome at all, made
A curious three-some.

Archie rode no side door
Pullmans; was too young
For World War II; missed
Korea and no Feds came
Into the classroom made
Him for a Commie. Rock
And acid, punk and metal,
Glam and rap passed him
By. Vietnam, too. Through
Entire eras, he wore
Dumb sweaters and carried
Some girl's books. The
Three of them got make-
Overs every generation but
It never fooled me.

Betty will forever contribute
The baked goods, marry a
Mason named Herb. They'll
Have three blonde daughters
Who'll harmonize about Jesus
Loving them when company comes
Over. They're not allowed
To mention 'Aunt' Veronica.

Ever. She and Archie won't
Be living in *that*
Neighbourhood.
She broke the heart of the
Football hero. It's her
Jughead summoned on those
Long suburban nights
In his room, walls hung with
Pennants, on his back
On his bed.

She'll lead Archie a merry
Chase. Starting age fifteen
Veronica stole away to motels
With grown-up men; it was
Her you saw, leaning back
Tight skirt, cashmere sweater,
Rumpled bed. Archie
Or some other guy
Lighting a smoke, on all
Those paperback covers.

She'll stay up late drinking
With Archie, Coleman Hawkins
On the radio but get up
In the dawn, slip out of
The room, heels in hand, and
Take the short; come back
Three weeks later, no
Explanations. Archie won't
Say a thing; he'd
Better not. It's Veronica's
Got what he's always needed.
She's had that since they
First met, seventy-six
Years ago, when they were

Just a couple of star-
Crossed kids, and they
Still are.

That flat shoes,
Subdivision, Pepsodent smile
Blonde, she was never really
In the game at all.

Tucumcari Roadhouse

Limping up to the Tucumcari
Roadhouse in a '51 Lincoln, low-
Slung, charcoal-primer, Autumn
1966.
Stretched my legs at a wooden
Booth. Fed quarters to the box.
Solomon and Otis answered. And
The waitress emerged,
A shade from the shadow world,
The other side of the swinging kitchen
Door. The angel of the scrubland,
Her eyes the colour of my car
But death in there. Plates
Ranked along her arms. She
Gave me a medieval look and went
Off, white shoes and long legs, with
My order. I thought of her underwear,
And moments stolen in the trailer
Out back. Wolves would pause
And howl on their way into Paris
When she brought out the knife.

Next day she'd stuff a cardboard
Suitcase and catch the Hound
For Santa Fe. It would be three
Weeks until I was found, just
Enough skin that a smile
Could be seen instead of a grimace.

I left the money on the table,
And with a smirk, she crossed herself
And watched me go. I started
The Lincoln and broadcast gravel leaving,
One arm out the window,
The other hand gripping tightly
The suicide knob.

List of Contributors

Taylor Cheoweth teaches creative writing at McDill University

And

Digby Todd teaches creative writing at Haldousie University

And

Marsha Manners teaches creative writing at Slocan University

And

Sanford Murchison is head of the Creative Writing School at Blanders University

And

Kerry Farnsworth is a student in the Creative Writing Department at Blanders University

And

Abdou Mahouf treaches creative writing at Dunvegan University (although with a name like that one might, perhaps, have expected something different)

And

Rodney Finkledown teaches creative writing at Dead Deer College

And

Sidney Westmoreland teaches creative writing at Humphries University

And

Martin Culpepper is president of the Society of Creative Writing Teachers of Canada (SCWTC)

And

Byron Fipps teaches creative writing at Yellowknife School of the Arts

And
Lisa Nullafoid teaches creative writing at the
   University of Osoyoos, at Oliver
And
Len Gasparini drives a truck.

The Lady on Radio Road

As if God had dropped his dice
On a dead man's overcoat gone
Green with age, rolling and rock
Strewn is the country hereabouts
And a drama's unfolding in each
Handsome, hand-wrought house,
No doubt.

But the brooks don't taddle
And what's done shouldn't matter.
Nevertheless, we all wonder
About the lady on Radio Road.

Like someone out of a mystery book
With her strange and foreign look
And that dark-eyed, thousand yard stare.
She just appeared out of nowhere.

Wheeling that ancient ragtop Packard,
She must have come many a weary mile
And with an iron skeleton key
Let herself in to the haunted Psalmanazer pile
On a night when the old moon was sitting
In the lap of the new.

Perhaps she's related to the ancient woman
That up and disappeared
Or that old man – he used to strip naked
And run through the thorny ash
Calling on Jesus. Whatever became of him?

But I don't care about any of that
She's my only concern, stays
Out there all alone
The lady on Radio Road.

Of course, there's a veritable riot of rumour
Like the one about the inoperable tumour
Or Spanish millions buried in the yard.

Now I heard it from a company insider –
He works for the provider – that
She's got no internet there.

An aloof but exotic thing
She wears a diamond and ruby ring
But on the third finger of the other hand.
I've never seen her with a man.
And she get's no mail except bills.
She's the only one for 50 kilometres around
That didn't come to town
The night of the Volunteer Firefighters ball.

Surely she must get bored
When she's done her chores.
No one ever comes to call.
She mustn't have any friends, at all.
Just a rooster and hens, a fat
Yellow duck and a donkey called Old Ben.

In the pale moonlight
On long summer nights
She sits quietly on the porch
Listening to birds roosting in the gorse
And sings those old Berlin songs.

In the winter it's different
She stays in the kitchen
In an original Eames chair.
There's an old radio there
And it's in a wooden cabinet
That's taller, they say, than
Her son when he ran away.
There's some kind of magic
She brings to that dark antique box
To coax out those radio waves
From the past.
They floated for who knows
How long up there
In the ethereal air
Until summoned by the lady
On Radio Road.

> Good evening, and who knows what evil
> Lurks in the hearts of men
> And women, too.
>
> The taxis tonight went out to the Marne
>
> And cops while making their rounds
> Almost found that elusive him
> Called Seldom Seen Slim
>
>> Meanwhile, the Allies have cooked
>>   Mussolini's goose.
>> And now, here's Bird
>> Live from the Royal Roost

Until the wee small hours
She stays right there.
Is she content in her famous chair

With radio visions from another age?
Or is she doting over every page
In her scrapbook of regrets?

Wouldn't she finally just rather forget?
Only the Shadow knows for sure.

Unhappy, willing or resigned
Would that she'd give me a sign:
A lantern on the cracked leather seat
Of the dead John Deere
Or the tail of a possum hanging
From the Chinaberry tree.
The flag turned up on her mailbox
Would be best of all – with a note
Inside for me.

Life needn't be so hard.
I don't care
About any Spanish doubloons
Buried in the yard.
Life needn't be so sad.
I'd treasure every stolen
Moment that I had

With the lady
On Radio Road.

A Hundred Acres and Some Kind of Fool

They expect to see plans for two
Thousand townhouses and a taproom
On every corner. To them plowed
Fields could be stripes on a fat man's
Zootsuit; green rolling hills a snake
Writhing beneath pool table felt; and
Don't the wetlands look like bourbon
Spilled in an ashtray at three A.M.?

One subway refugee brought me
An album from early doo wop days but
I already have Ravens, Robins, Orioles
And the Red-breasted Grosbeaks.

The bull and his cows stay
On one side of the electric fence
And me on the other. I got no
Television but watch deer
At the crepuscular hour
And later stare heavenward
In the million-noted night. True,
I miss the Racing Form
But I named the gimpy donkey
Silky Sullivan. No one comes
Swaggering onto my turf
Shirttails out to cover
Any waistband bulges
Just a guy about the Septic
Tank and another in a Cardinals

Cap to trap the beaver pond.
When they complain about the quiet
I tell them, "Hey, you should
Have been here the other day when
Three-finger Sal was hiding
In the barn. And only last week
Baldhead Perkins ran off screaming
Through the bull rushes."

They must go back to the city, say
I've lost my edge. "Next thing
You know, he'll be writing goddamn
Nature poems. Or maybe he's just
Playing a part, like his hero,
Willie the Actor."

Let them have their illusions. I'm
Staying right here, tossing
Cow patties at the moon,
At least until the whole thing
Blows over.

Strip Bar Haiku

Signs in the window:

Topless!

Bottomless!

I hurry inside.

There's no one there.

Funny Old Memory

What would your parents say
If they knew you were seeing
A guy my age? *Say*? What
Would they *do*? Summon
The Mounties? Call out
The dogs of war? Or
A protestant minister
In a cheap suit to
Pray for me? If I
Dated your mother
I'd be keeping company
With a much younger woman.
So what does this say
About me and you?

I don't care as long
As you come over here
And do what you do. My
Cinnamon, my nectarine,
My soft ice cream.

Your ex-boyfriend wears
A hoodie, knows you have
Someone else but he doesn't
Know who. Maybe he'll come
Gunning for me
In his daddy's car. Where's
He going to look first, the
Mall? Dude's gonna be
Some kind of surprised.
If you see him, set him

Straight. It's about quality
Not frequency.

You keep loving me the way
You do and I just might do
Your homework for you.

You're the darling buds of May
And I'm crusty December but no
Ice has formed around my heart.

Have all my hair,
I'm not a physical wreck.
Got a washboard stomach
And a pension cheque.

And you have the softest neck
And rubbery skin, like
I never dreamed
I'd ever feel again.

And you have all
The world and all
Its time, and this moment
For you will turn
Into just some
Funny old
Memory.

Wooden Indians

Scattered in the long ago across
North America, a great nation,
More numerous than Kiowa,
Ottawa, Pawnee, Comanche
And never took to the warpath.
Where did they go, those wooden
Indians? In my childhood, an old
Deciduous one on Sycamore Street
Had stood shaggy and immobile
Through The Siege of Petersburg, the big
Band era and early-Elvis.
There was a big one at Fat Annie's roadhouse
In *Pete Kelly's Blues*. Some were
Famous, like poor ol' Kawliga but most
Nameless old warriors who had buried the hatchet
To stand all dignified out front of cigar stores.
Where did they go?

Maybe they were rounded up in the middle
Of the night and transported to thoroughly
Inappropriate camps, like Geronimo
Sent to Florida to rot in the humidity? Were
They shanghaied for figureheads on
Clipper ships? Maybe they were massacred
By black plaster lawn jockeys. Somewhere
There are wooden Indians in warehouses,
Wrapped in termite blankets. They've
Even removed wooden Indians
From museum dioramas where they hunted
Paper mâché buffalo. I dreamed
There's a lost nation still of wooden

Indians. Many, I'm told,
Fled to Europe like jazzmen.
They get no respect.
If a movie were ever made about wooden Indians,
They'll probably be played by wooden Italians.
They have no status, file no claims, yet
Most white people boast of having some
Wooden Indian blood, usually Cherokee, but
They don't invite them into their homes.
Tell the truth, would you let your daughter
Go out with a wooden Indian? Wouldn't
You worry he'd always be hard?
I heard the ones who remain are being forced
To assimilate by marrying ventriloquists'
Dummies. Be kind to the next
Wooden Indian you see for, after all,
Maybe he doesn't really
Have a wooden heart.

Camilo's Bitch

Maybe you've seen me,
One good eye staring
Into the lens, being patted
By Fidel or Che or Benny
More. But I belonged, finally,
To Cienfuegos who one-handed,
Grabbed me from the gutter, my
Right eye gone, left leg nearly
Severed by a machete in the paw
Of a Batista bully boy. Camilo
Who like Camillus dressed my
Wound, soothed my suppurating
Eye hole and fed me from
A Bucanero bottle. He carried
Me along the Southern Route
And up into the Sierra Maestre
Where I learned to walk again,
And did beside my companeros,
Like a baby brindle burro,
Sugar and cigars in my little
Saddle bags. I was all colours
Like the people of our nation. I
Knew when to bark and when
To hold my tongue. For days
The men did not eat,
Nor me.

I was seen by gringos in newsreels
The day we took Havana. I loved
Camilo's anarchist ways, he
Was Malatesta with a khaki cap
And gun. I tried to keep him

From climbing the stairs
To that plane. I growled and nipped,
And tugged at his cuffs, the
Camouflaged cotton between
My pointy teeth, and growled,
And Fidel laughed;
Nervously, I thought. And Camilo
Told me Hasta Luego. But I knew
There'd be no later.

"Pobrecita, probrecita!" the neighbours
Said to me. My master dead
At thirty-three, who'd fed
Me from a bottle. Well, I lived on
For years and years in the home
Of a singer of sones and sols,
Boleros, too. People came
To take my picture, the one-
Eyed dog with the crooked leg
Who'd known them all. And
When I died, not shot
By bureaucrats, alas, but
Of distemper, and bad temper
At what could have been, they
Stuffed me, and for years I rode
On the back seats of limousines
And was too much stroked
By Slavs in cheap suits
And nervous Canadians. I lost
My multi-coloured coat
And withered just like
The Revolution but still I
Stared up at Fidel, now
With two eyes of marble and
A question in each. My pointy
Teeth still bared.

And Let the Games End

He spent opening day without
Ceremony over by the hard luck
Jukebox in a huddle with other
Athletes of his era, before
Four sleeves of lager, blond
And identical like all
His ex-wives.
What a raw talent he'd been!
Still sits at the top
Of the record book for getting
To the bottom in the least
Amount of time. He continually
Jumped the gun in his zeal
To outdistance responsibility.
It was the synchronized events
Put paid to any dreams of glory.
He can't even remember the faces
Of teammates who'd depended
On him.
While skating the real
Problems, he, nevertheless,
Fell through the ice of life.
Yet, still he carries the torch;
Three or 4, in fact.
And when the Games are over
He'll hobble back to Loser's
Village, turn up the volume
On a TV set that is, alas,
High definition, dig out
The nine millimetre from
The cardboard box of trophies

That he awarded himself, and aim
To make the Evening News.

Early Music

Not clavichorded nor with
Clavicle bones beat on
Hollow Mississippi stumps
But Hank Williams in
The Virginia sideyard by
The smokehouse. "Hey, Good
Lookin" coming though
The open summer window,
Floating over cherry cherry
Pies cooling on the sill
In 2/4 time from out
The kitchen. Whatcha got
cooking? Would have been six
Years old 1951, playing probably
Cowboys and Indians.
On the hard road, cross
The cornfield, a hotrod Ford
Headed right over the hill Howsa
Bout a ... howsabouta ...
Howsabouta ...
With me?

Even-toed Ungulates

Oh, these even-toed
Ungulates, they only seem
Haughty, at first. Note
The twinkle in the big eye
Veiled by Theda Bara lashes.
Makes me think of gangly
Upper class ladies, like
Eleanor Roosevelt with flat
Foot walk and clumpy shoes
Who don't know they're funny.
I thought one was John Diefenbaker.
Someone got them drunk
And put bracelets on their ankles.
They're sweet unless you
Cross them.

Fortunes having fallen
From wild desert days, they
Must pull groaning carts
Of rebar along Rathambor
Roads and entire nomad
Families of entertainers
Across Rahjastan.
But the magicians
Cannot transport them
To Saharan vastness, as
Humiliated as cobras in baskets
De-fanged, de-poisoned, riding
In back of the hump that can
Only puff up impotently.
Camels all decorated, same

As other beasts and buses,
With Lakshmi on the dash
Board, Shiva guards the bumpers.
Here the bulls have painted horns
To mock any Hemingways. I
Saw an elephant in white face
With blue and red polka dots.
But camels all caparisoned steal
The ever-moving show, festooned
With moon rays, sun rays and stars.
Stick figures roam their flanks.
One dares sport ganesha on
A shoulder; another has its own
Camel; lift the corner of
The saddle to see Kama Sutra
Copulations. One is zig-zag
Shaven and another has a coat
Like Mike Tyson's head. From
The noggin of that beast at
Bangalore and dyed black, hair-
Fur sprouted like a boomtown
Gusher.

Don't misunderstand them
There is no water in those
Humps. "Camel" means
Beauty.

Bus Ride

Transmission whine like a wounded
Hound of hell. Gears grind call to mind
A choking man. The driver thinking
Of his wife while advising: "This
Is Cincinnati … Saskatoon … Medicine Bow
Or Medicine Hat … It's
Your meal stop, folks …We'll
Be here half an hour … remember
The number of your bus …"

Muncho Lake at 1AM, all huddled like foot
Ballers around the oil drum stove, eating
Champion cinnamon buns while the green
Water wears its winter cloak and
Crouches down behind trees, hiding
In the night.

The coffee in Truckee weaker
Than the promises of the one back
In Reno who made jokes about having
Our own Donner Party but didn't
Show up at the station.

Bus left me lollygagging in Florence,
South Carolina and while peeing forty
Years later near Buon Mai
Tout, Vietnam.

Decades that glimpsed my face
In a thousand sliding back windows
Looking through nights scattered

With stars and lights in rooms
Of stay-at-homes. The old man
Just come in from the woodpile
Lights his pipe. Ma carries from
The kitchen the apple pie like his
Crown on a satin pillow. They'll
Look outside later, predict tomorrow's
Weather, and see the bus but not care
It's there or where it's going.

Looking through them to dawn in
Middle Florida, dogs under porches
Raised on pilings, yawning, content
Not to be Greyhounds, and palm fronds
Scratch rusted rooftop eczema
Of decrepit automobiles.

Looked through them later at clouds
Like fingerprints. Curlicues of smoke
From fires signaling breakfast
In Manitoba, Rajasthan, ranch house
West of Butte, rowhouse
In rainy Namur.

Looking through them on into the after-
Noon of the side-of-the-highway world;
All the vacant towns of America; brown
Indians bent over in white farm fields
On stolen Red Indian land.

Back of the bus interracial romance. In
North Carolina I kissed her starfish
Lips. In Massachusetts I held Emily
Dickinson on my lap, the flimsy
Toilet door flapping, a black
Guy at the front rapping

About winter things, some mythical
Trickster brother on skis
At Colorado Springs.

Off the grand, plush seat Mexican
Bus to cross the trickle of brown
Rio Grande into a third world-like
U.S.A. The tired Trailways and
The tired driver's drug and gun warning.
On past Brownsville graveyard, tombstones
Make a tenement skyline. That day, March 5
Marked her birth date, stars big
And bright in the layer cake night. She's
Sleeping eternity second from the left,
Third row back from the road.

On first bus across the Peten, Mayan
Ladies hid me under blankets and plastic
Shopping bags as sten gun revolutionaries,
Dark-eyed bandits, really, in balaclavas,
Searched for foreigners or others with
Money.

Passing the black baby hand to hand
Like a hotdog at the ball park to
The back of the Bluebird in Belize.

The reading light on in Wyoming, funnel
To a world more alien than Sulawesi
To pistol-packing seat mate; turning pages
Through Sinclair, Rawlins, Rock Springs
And didn't even look up at Wamsutter.

And what about a thousand other
Seat mates?

Me, I'm going to Fort Nelson got
A job in the bush. Hope it's far enough
Back, I'll forget her there.

    Me, I just ride the bus all over, all
The time. I'm 76, got no family, nothing
Else to do.

    Me, I'm going home to Indiana, near
Vincennes. My Daddy's funeral.

    Me, I'm headed back to Estevan, marry
My girl. I got her picture right here.

    Me, I'm just out of jail. They bought
My ticket home.

    Me, I'm not rightly sure where I'm going
But I'm sure it sure as hell don't matter.

And how about you, Bud?

> "This is Dawson Creek, folks. Your
> Meal stop. We'll be here half an hour …
> Remember the number
> Of your bus … "

One Gaunt White Man

One gaunt white man
Blowing two notes
On a harmonica
Over and over
And over again.
Always on Granville
Same spot East of
Eaton's, south
Of the Birks clock.
Looked like Artaud
In the later years
And younger than he
Looked. Two notes
Over and over
And over again
But with the occasional
Two-bar break for a
"Hey, man" or "Thanks,
Hunh" though nobody
I ever noticed
But for me and
One small Bengali
Woman gave him
Money.
Better than anyone
I ever saw at the
Commodore, half
A block away.
Stomping his right
Foot on wet pavement.
Big boot sprayed rain

Water, harmonica mouth
Sprayed spittle. He
Found it, he had it.
Where did he go?
"Hey, man …
Thanks, hunh."

Where to, Zoe?

Where to, Zoe? Four
In the morning, club just
Closed down, looking like
A beachfront ballroom on
A winter dawn, and the steroid
Bouncer's some police force
Reject. He knows you
By now, spared you waiting
Out front like some beggar
In a food bank line. That
Was hours ago, now he just
Wants to follow you home.
Zoe pictures him washing down
His Cialis with a human
Growth hormone power shake.
There were others:
The lawyer who bought you
Martinis, wanted you to fish
Out the olive with your tongue,
Suck on it. A developer offered
You blow. Said he got it
From a guy he knows
In the Andes.
Well, a suburban
Kid just walked into a wall
And apologized. The neon's
Passed out and the moon's
Drowning in a puddle. Here's
A taxi. Try the unusual,
Zoe. Go home.
It's early if you're a milkman

Or it would be if they still
Had them. The driver says
He's from Yemen. Has six kids
And supports an uncle back home
That lives in a sand dune or
Something. Well, dude, we all
Have problems. Watch
What you tell him, Zoe, or
He might drive into the Lake, for
Spite, or bomb your building, like
That would be a loss. What to do
Now – 4:08 – sum up the evening
In twenty-four characters? Maybe
Somebody knows a new club. This
One's been around five months, so
Long Zoe's shoes have gone out of
Style; it should be a heritage site.
God, she sighs, and the driver
Says, "Miss?" But she ignores him.
There's nothing happening. Read
A book? What a laugh. Who has
Time? 4:11. Hours 'til the first
Latte, and the shops open. Zoe,
You wondered once, it was just
For a moment, maybe a month ago,
What it's all about and what do
You have that's your own. Forget
Innocence, and she almost has, it's
Like the shadow of a dream as you're
Waking. Even the name is fake.
She's really Marsha but Zoe,
It sounds so cute, gamine-like.
Yes, what next, Zoe? In the mirror
She saw a line, what, a week ago?
Still not yet for lipo-suction.
Don't need no breast enhancement,

Not with these puppies. Maybe a bum
Lift at one of those resorts where
They have latte-coloured towel
Boys. That's it: Gonna have me
A bum lift holiday.
Yes, well, where's that girl-
Hood white horse hero? He's
No towel boy or rent-a-bouncer,
Either. Maybe the new version
Is a developer with China White
Or a Horse habit. Would she ever
Recognize the real him
If he appeared? Maybe he's
Omar up there, brown eyes
In the rearview.
> The night is so lonely, is it
> Not, Miss? We travel through
> It sometimes as if hungry dogs
> With tails between our legs,
> Other times like rabid curs
> Who only wish to pass on our
> Illness. It's all a mystery,
> Truly. Wider than the desert
> Back home. We look for answers
> In all the wrong places because
> All places are the wrong ones.
> There is no relief except with
> One another –

Oh, God, here it comes, thinks Zoe.
> – Well, good night,
> Miss. I hope tomorrow is better
> For you. May the daylight bring
> You honey and dates, and a pleasant
> Breeze that carries a message
> Of good fortune.

Yeah, well, whatever, thinks
Zoe, and holds back part
Of his tip for being presumptuous
And not knowing she could
See through that middle-eastern
Mystic routine of his.

Her building there, it looks
Like a cigarette lighter in
The sunshine but a tall tombstone
Now. The elevator grumbles
Like a camel. Mix one last drink,
Zoe. Lay back in the recliner.
Click on the shopping channel,
Reach under your skirt and wait
For the stores to open.

Our First Night at the Buchan

We made our escape
Before the authorities had been
Alerted, and before we heard
Each other's story. You were
Probably making up yours
On the ferry over. The windows
Of our Buchan room looked out
Over augury bushes. You took
Your shower first and used
Both towels; left them
On the wet tile floor. Me,
I dried myself with a pillow
Case, then dressed in my
Sunday best, and you were
In lingerie and we danced
Around the floor, like waltzing
Across Texas with all
The time in the world. And
From our whirling bodies sparks
Shot silvery, like swords on
A grindstone wheel. I dreamed
Bamboo grew along a billabong
And I was the boy in the song,
Skipping along inside the dawn.
Your butterscotch shoulders
Made up my whole golden
Horizon. I got a mouthful
Of Fool's Gold when I prospected
There. Your eyes glittered like
Fireflies looking for the evening's
Mate. They saw inside me and

Through. You had me coming
And going. You melted in my arms
My jelly belly, my jujube. You
Lead from the beginning; a merry
Dance it was. And I realized
Too late the fate those
Two towels foretold.

Big Nicky

Big Nicky hung head down,
Like Mussolini, from the water
Pipes in the Ninth Street Garage,
Thinking to stretch his spine while
Rats tried to nibble the dangling
Wings of his duck's ass, and we,
What passed as his pals, peeked
Through greasy windows, feeling
Like we shouldn't be. Me,
Embarrassed, tried to figure how
They got the wire in the glass.
Big Nicky would stand on his toes
In box camera snapshots. In pegged
Pants, satin shirt and elevator
Shoes, Big Nicky was dressed up never
Vined down. He lied about his height
And was mean about it, quick as
Cyrano to take offense but without
The wit, and maidens in those parts
Weren't made for poetry under
The balcony, only subdivisions
Over swamps in South Jersey. He
Was like that grease pit Alsatian,
Dripping saliva on anyone looked
At him peculiar.
Meanwhile, four blocks away
Outside Mob territory, other side
Of what was called the Zambesi – I
Thought that was Italian
For Third Street – in another
Land, lived Little Thomas, bigger

Than any other kid, and black
And placid as old rainwater
In an asphalt puddle until
Ruffled by a tire that wasn't
Paying attention. Came the day
Big Nicky went strutting
Into that foreign territory
And there sat Little Thomas
On his stoop, bottle of Frank's
Cream soda, chocolate Tastycake
Cupcakes, scanning ball scores.
For Joe Black shutouts, Willie
Mays basket catches, seeing Luke
Easter towering four-baggers
On the fourth of July. Little
Thomas looks up, sees Big
Nicky, digs his threads, says,
Smiling, "My, you do look sporty" only
Big Nicky thinks he hears, "Hey, you,
Shorty!" and quicker than
The crack of a bat, Nicky
Is off his leash, going
For Little's throat with parrot claw
Hands. But the big kid lifted
The little kid and flung him
Like a medicine ball against
The front of the car at the curb,
And the 88's hood rocket launched
Into the spine Big Nicky was always
Trying to stretch. Still, he got
The stiletto from his pegged pants
Pocket, and then it was as if
Little Thomas hit him
With the rest of the Oldsmobile.

Big Nicky spent the remainder
Of his life on his side
In a kind of playpen, specially
Fabricated and elongated.
He was mostly paralyzed but
Could wiggle two fingers, slowly
Like a shy man signaling
For a another drink, and he was
Good at bending the bottom leg back
Quickly, like a dog covering
Up his business. He could
Roll his eyes and talk, too.
Big Nicky was the older brother
Of Loretta with whom I
Skipped school to cross
The wide Oregon Avenue and ride
Junkyard horses in west Texas.
She fed Big Nicky, and their
Mother changed his adult-size diapers.
When I brought new kids over, he'd
Assure them that only since he'd
Been attacked had his body shriveled
And twisted. He was like a snake
Coiled in a cage, that could only
Hiss.

> "I would have been six-two, 6'
> 1" easy" he'd declare between
> Spoons full of his sister's
> Applesauce and maybe a little
> Panetone soaked in milk at
> Christmas time, "if it weren't
> For those mamelukes."

Big Nicky lived to be 41 years old
And they say he died cursing.

Little Thomas got five for
Big Nicky, and was 18 when
Rizzo's cops came through
The front door, firing. They
Put 34 slugs into him and his
Sister who were eating in
Front of the television at the time,
Watching 'Willie the Worm'. Cops
Had the wrong house.

Greenberg's Drugstore

He looked like he should be
In the aisle with the toys, his
Head lower than the top shelf
Teddybears. Then you saw the liver
Spots peeking through his thinning
Hair, Greenberg, an old baby regarding
You through Barney Google glasses,
Spraying you like a cracked garden hose.
I drove his Volkswagen van, first one
I'd ever seen, 4-speed standard.
Greenberg's in green across the sides.

His assistant was named Jim, a
Japanese druggist who claimed to be
Hawaiian, the war over only sixteen
Years. His hair was like a neglected
Lawn in a forgotten neighbourhood
In a science-fiction film where
The flora is all black. He didn't
Like me. I must have resembled hillbilly
Yokohama occupiers. Soon it was
Mutual.

I did like making deliveries for measle-ly
Children, hapless hypochondriacs and Mrs.
Entwhistle. First day, I held out the white
Bag with the receipt stapled across
The fold, she reached out and grabbed
My zipper instead. She was old, probably
Forty but smelled good. She did something
With the tip of her tongue that, not

Surprisingly, I'd never experienced
(still haven't). Two days a week,
I'd park the van out front of her
house – mail box on a wagon wheel
In a bed of geraniums, garden gnome,
He resembled Mr. Greenberg, guarding
The door – She always asked if
I had some medicine for her. She
Took to wearing dark red lipstick,
And always wanted two doses.

Back at the store, Greenberg took to calling
Me Little Jim and the fake Hawaiian Big Jim.
But I was tall enough to look down on his
Abandoned crew cut. He told the boss that
I looked at girlie magazines when I should
Be stocking shelves. It wasn't true. I'd
Think of Mrs. Entwhistle, and didn't need
Magazines. The last time he told Greenberg,
I overheard and demanded it wasn't true.
"Little Jim, you say Big Jim is lying?" –
And I said he was. He had to let me go
Because he couldn't have any animosity
But I could tell he believed me.

I couldn't very well go to Mrs. Entwhistle's
House without the delivery van though I got
As far as the wagon wheel one time
But was brought up short by the look
On the garden gnome's face. The lady
Of the house would have to
Get her medicine
From somebody else.

Another Round

"Haven't seen you since the Seventies," the old
Bartender said, reaching out a hand that shook
Like a bad actor overdoing it in a movie. "It
Sure was great to be young in Toronto back then,
Eh?" As he looked at me, marveling, no doubt,
At how I'd aged, I told him it would have been great
To be young anywhere. His eyes put me in mind
Of ice cubes melting in a glass, turning
Bourbon cloudy. "What memories," he added.
"What A decade!"
Oh, sure, I thought. It was great, particularly
Those rented rooms where you were never alone,
All your predecessors wanted in
The bed, and despair was the gargoyle
Crouching in the closet. All the hardluck
Stories, given a Turkish or Latvian twist,
Shared in double-burner hot plate kitchens.

There were women who threw things and didn't
Always miss. The one who had burned half a
Manuscript by the time I got back from
The liquor store and would have finished
The job if I hadn't had her favourite:
Sweet red vermouth, darker than her
Lips – 474B.

Nor would nostalgia be so sweet without
Memories of guys waiting in parking
Lots, jumping up like jacks in boxes
From behind cars. The guy with the knife,
So rusted and thick the blade, it

Might have come from a tomb in Peru,
And he a mean, inbred archaeologist.
The easiest was the guy with the nunchaka sticks
On Brunswick Avenue.

And cops. Getting my head
And shoulders beat with clubs
For just being there. Anywhere.
The three who were dragging my girl
Friend into the alley when I showed up.
One with his zipper
Already down.

And the wonderful jobs, the Cherry Street
Drill press, boring holes to be filled by bolts
Forever. Nails banged, lawns mown.
The Etobicoke stamping
Machine that seemed
To be canceling my days
One after another.

But, still, you know, the wine
Was good and I could always
Find a song, and there was the
"And all that" that old bartender
Mentioned. And all that
Going away and coming back.
The rich palette of eye
Shadow; thin straps that
Surrounded trim ankles in high
Heel shoes. The limbs, all
colours. Bracelets that rattled
Like beaded curtains to back rooms.
The back rooms.

Forty-one cents in the Metro Café, Bathurst
And Bloor, and not caring; watching
The red-haired Christian Science hooker
Ply her trade. The Chinese grill man
With the rockabilly pompadour, flipping
Flapjacks in the Crest Diner. Guy
With burlesque scrapbook in his
Room above the Victory, turning pages
Like a librarian with a medieval manuscript
Of illuminated buxom saints.
Jack Gummerson in the middle of the back
Yard on the first daffodil morning, three
Drinks into the bottle singing about
The rain drops falling
On his head.
And lying in bed in the dark
Of a thick summer's night, Carleton
Street just back from Namibia,
Listening to the old lion roar
At the old zoo in the ravine, wondering
If he was asking if Africa was still
As he remembered it, oh, so long ago.

Well, okay, old bartender, you were right
Afterall. It was particularly great to be
Young then and there, and now
I feel like that old lion. So why don't you
Bring me another round of the Seventies.
I had them too fast, the last
Time.

Runagate Again

The taxi dancer gave me a lift,
Dropped me off at the border,
And I was in the wind. I timed
The searchlights, crawled through
Barbed wire like an eager doughboy
And made for the aspidistra. There
Are interdictions about this
Sort of thing but I had to have
A look-see like any good newshound.
So I made my way across the fabled
Lobotomy hills and slept the sleep
Of the truly frightened there
At the edge of the outer plague
Precincts and next morning under
A Vaseline sky along polenta-coloured
Streets, I skulked into town. A big
Screen at the end of every thoroughfare
Like a backstop displayed the Supreme
Arbiter in a gaily painted gasmask
Observing his flock
FOR THEIR OWN GOOD.

Hereabouts rumour had announced
A preponderance of arch fiends
And it – Rumour – wasn't whistling
Dixie, Jack. You had to be
Up to date, buff and work on your apps.
Get atomic downloads and vivisection
Porno. No history here, they'd
Already run the classics out of town.

Cyclops was over at customs getting
A retinal scan. Diogenes made it in,
His face disguised with lampblack. Even
Ibn Batutta had paused, hiding in
The tropaeolium, for a gander.
It was a place where even certitudes
Had to toe the line. In the public
Evisceration chambers through loud
Speakers the authoritarian corps
Like Max Beckmann boys
Cracked wise and troglodytes sang
Torch songs.
Law? There was no law, Buddy.
Why the whole inbred lot of them
Persisted in denying Weismannism.
There was blood lust coursing through
The avenues. They gave the Iron Cross
To mono-metalists.
Wolverines took over the foot
Bath and idolaters became the new gods.
I tell you it was a gerrymandered land
Of vast and multitudinous gimcrackery.
The Chinese wore chinos.
Here, for sure, no amelioration of angels
Would ever take place. The vicar was no help.
He spiffed a Gibraltar ape who worked
In the bank and they were both busted
For simony. To tell the truth,
I didn't understand a thing
And my dragoman had been lulled to sleep
By the obfuscation girls.
They tried to buy me off
By fixing me up
But all she'd ever be to me
Was a sexed up simulacrum

Of love long lost. I appeared
At her door at Xmas time with
A red nose and a colourful sobriquet.
She had jabot at her bodice
And smelled of muscadine.
We were serenaded by a choir
Of bright-eyed cajolers.
She led me in from the porch,
Lit a torch, turned the stereo
Low, offered me some blow,
Said, "Excuse me while I go
And slip into something
Uncomfortable."
She returned in chain mail,
Postage overdue, and carrying
Before her, three strap-ons,
Like championship belts, and said,
"Which one, Ducky?"
My sweet nothings came to naught.
Neither my primulas or my probity.
"Prink as you might," she said.
"But if you stay be it known
That sooner or later you'll
Have to assume the procumbent
Position."
Well I got out of there all right
And lit out for the lobotomy hills,
Rested by a poisoned lake just
The ticket for my lucubrations,
And gained the aspidistra where I
Offered up my profound conjurations.
Stuck in the barbed wire were
Three guys, all milk brothers, mewling
For their mothers.

But I got through and my dear Taxi
Dancer was waiting. She'd kept
The motor running and the radio on.
They were playing my song
And I sang along:
"Hallelujah, I'm a runagate
Again."

Tiger Man

That Mess-with-me at-your-peril,-Bud
Look, malevolent twinkle in cracker eyes, as
If he knew what would happen if you did.
Coming into second like a maniac pilot
Landing on a jungle strip, top leg
At forty-five Degrees, filed spikes sparkling
In the sun of red dirt, green grass day games:
My first god – Ty Cobb. The greatest
There'd ever been or ever will be. Top
Of the list in all categories from
Bases to bastards. Hero, too; running
Down Detroit streetcars to pull off hooligans
Who'd mugged old ladies, and he left
Them bleeding on the pavement. Made
A million off a cocaine-laced soft drink.
But received jeers not Ruthian cheers.

And that's the guy I wanted to be
Just like. Aped his style and moves but
Was neither bad enough nor good
Enough. Couldn't ever deal
With the curves thrown at me. My
Record notable not for hits but
Misses. When there were spikes
Women were wearing them
And the money I never made
Was the file that sharpened them.
I stumbled on the basepaths, fell
For the hidden ball trick, balked
At responsibilities, and if I ever stole
A single heart it was surely
Unintentional.

Afternoon of the Blind Man

He smelled me coming, my friend
The blind man. I was there to
Back him up and pick him up. Time
Is precious, he said. Let us go
Before the care giver comes. I
Guided the lab into the bedroom.
The blind man flung his cane, shattering
The lamp guests used, and bolted from
The house, like a horse without
Blinders from a barn on fire. Of
Course, he tumbled down the stairs
But got up laughing, for this
Was his big day. He took off
Running, in white hat, shades,
Referee shirt, red and gold brocade
Vest. "Doesn't that guy have a
Mirror?" someone exclaimed. He looked
Like a zebra with a gypsy saddle.
And he galloped along Fort Street,
Scattering the sighted. The blind
Man dashed into Maisonneuve, got
Clipped by a yellow cab, tripped
Over a curb and was flung into
The big window of Pharma Prix.
Sitting in a puddle of glass, he
Wanted to know what happened. When
I told him, he wanted to know
What glass is, really. "And what
Is a window? Taxi cab?
Zebra? Woman's flesh? And
When they look at me with pity,
What does that look like?"

He took off again. Me jogging
Behind all afternoon to help
Him up when he fell. He smashed
A knee on Guy. Upended a
Haitian on Côte-des-Neiges,
Bumped into another blind man
On Peel Street, and was halfway
Up the mountain before they
Nabbed him. "What is a mountain?" he
Demanded of ambulance attendants, and
They answered, "Now, now."

Officials placed his hand where he had
To sign and turned him over
To the Directorate of the Blind.
His cane was retrieved, so
Was his dog. Immediately someone
Began to teach him a craft he
Hadn't learned yet. And a serious
Man showed up with the goatee
They all seem to have
And wanted to know why. The blind
Man laughed and they told him,
"There is software to help you."

Guardalavaca Night

A silver caravel the moon
Makes against a demerara dark
Sky and sea. Two blue
Mahoes with truncated trunks
Flank a low barnacle wall
Bursting Bougainvillea,
And banana leaves like elephants'
Ears scratch my stingy brim.
It's like a tourist painting
But all of them have gone
Leaving only me, thinking
Of only you in this pre-revolutionary
Restaurant. Fluorescent tubes
Spread a cape of dim light over
The sand. Two cops loiter at
The hem of it, leaning against white
Beach loungers stacked to look
Like Port-a-Potties. Their talk sounds
Like Cuban machine guns but the palm
Fronds might as well be whispering
A windblown Ukrainian. They're in
The lee of a Kapok Kremona that might
Have been drawn by a tropical
Tot with a thick black crayola.
Now, if I hold the glass just so,
The breeze ruffles the dark liquid
And reflects the moon, that silver
Caravel that's taking me soon
Over demerara sky and sea
To you.

Forests

Toronto trees seen through trolley
Windows. Trunks patina-ed by exhaust
Smoke, bumper bashing, sparks, late-
Night pissers. Can't identify
Their species, same as passengers,
Without DNA bark or skin
Scratch samples.
         Sugar black Maple
         White pine Silver
         Ash Cedar green
         And the odd
                  Trembling Aspen

Like Somalian maybe mother there
With daughter part-Chinese or Buddha
Man, belly and breast drooping like
Too wet cement and cement coloured.
Her from Fiji, that Pakistani, he
Former king in Mali. What do they see
In windows? Trees, memories? Inside
Of Dundas car like Guyanese-Irian
Jayan-Javanese wing of Arboreum.

There's a little molly-coddled willow
Climbed by roses and pretty as
A peacock in the park.
A rare trio of acacias on a doctor's
Lawn, precious wispy like three
Australian girl singers
Doing the hand-jive far from home.

But don't weep for tough street trees,
Branches snarled in hydro wires. It
Beats being choked by bullies
Who throw their trunks around.
Poor trembling aspens smothered
By unruly Manitoba maples in
God's own forests out of town.

In city safe from chain saw massacres.
Don't trees realize
They'll live longer
On metropolitan streets
Like leopards in zoos or displaced
Persons.

ABOUT JIM CHRISTY'S PREVIOUS COLLECTIONS

"His poetry is like a cross between Catullus and a country song."
– *subTerrain Magazine*

"His voice is pure seduction."
– *Australian Broadcasting Company*

"A legendary figure."
– *Globe and Mail*

"An irrepressible adventurer and polymath."
– *Toronto Star*

"A Canadian Indiana Jones."
– *The National Enquirer*

"The most-widely travelled Canadian poet of his time."
– *Umbrella*

Printed in June 2013
by Gauvin Press,
Gatineau, Québec